THE LIFE
AND PRAYERS OF SAINT
AUGUSTINE

© **Wyatt North Publishing, LLC 2012**
A Boutique Publishing Company

Publishing by Wyatt North Publishing, LLC.

Copyright © Wyatt North Publishing, LLC. All rights reserved, including the right to reproduce this book or portions thereof in any form whatsoever. For more information please visit http://www.WyattNorth.com.

Cover design by Wyatt North Publishing, LLC. Copyright © Wyatt North Publishing, LLC. All rights reserved.

Scripture texts in this work are taken from the *New American Bible, revised edition*© 2010, 1991, 1986, 1970 Confraternity of Christian Doctrine, Washington, D.C. and are used by permission of the copyright owner. All Rights Reserved. No part of the New American Bible may be reproduced in any form without permission in writing from the copyright owner.

About Wyatt North Publishing

Starting out with just one writer, Wyatt North Publishing has expanded to include writers from across the country. Our writers include college professors, religious theologians, and historians.

Wyatt North Publishing provides high quality, perfectly formatted, original books.

Send us an email and we will personally respond with 24 hours! As a boutique publishing company we put our readers first and never respond with canned or automated emails. Contact us at hello@WyattNorth.com, and you can visit us online at www.WyattNorth.com

Foreword

The Church has numerous fathers who have influenced its dogma in substantial ways. Although none of them can be singled out as the most pivotal theologian of Church history, it can certainly be said that Saint Augustine of Hippo has long been a central figure to Christian thought, informing both on the nature of God and the nature of Christian morality.

He has been quoted throughout the ages by important Christian writers, such as Saint Thomas Aquinas, and has been listed as a strong influence by Pope Benedict XVI.

Through his central place in the history of Christianity, some historians have appointed Saint Augustine particularly great importance in European and World history. They have called him the last man of the Classical Age, and the first medieval man.

The Life of Saint Augustine

A thing is not necessarily true because badly uttered, nor false because spoken magnificently.

Introduction

The Church has numerous fathers who have influenced its dogma in substantial ways. Although none of them can be singled out as the most pivotal theologian of Church history, it can certainly be said that Saint Augustine of Hippo has long been a central figure to Christian thought, informing both on the nature of God and the nature of Christian morality.

He has been quoted throughout the ages by important Christian writers, such as Saint Thomas Aquinas, and has been listed as a strong influence by Pope Benedict XVI. Through his central place in the history of Christianity, some historians have appointed Saint Augustine particularly great importance in European and World history. They have called him the last man of the Classical Age, and the first medieval man.

An extremely prolific writer, Saint Augustine of Hippo produced more than one hundred titles in his lifetime. His works include great monoliths on the nature of God's grace, commentaries on scripture, books of doctrine, rebuttals to heresies, and sermons and letters.

He started writing even before he was a Christian, and started writing Christian works even before he was baptized. In many ways, he was a man of his time: well-read in ancient pagan poetry, philosophy, and rhetoric, deeply moved by the ascetic ideals of the fourth century.

Yet those same tendencies that mark him as so ordinary, also mark him as extraordinary. It is much thanks to Augustine that Greek thought, Neo-Platonism in particular, received its baptism, and was allowed to enter the Christian equation.

The most astonishing fact of the Blessed Augustine's life is perhaps how unlikely the Catholic Church was to find in him an ally and Doctor of the Church. In his younger years, Augustine directly opposed the Christian way of life, and he proselytized for other religions. He glorified pagan thinkers over the Scriptures, which he found coarse and unsophisticated. His resentment of the Church and Christian virtues was embodied by his often strained, and sometimes estranged, relationship with his Christian mother.

The main source on Saint Augustine's life is no doubt his

autobiographical work, <u>The Confessions</u>. Much can also be gleaned from his sermons, and his numerous letters, as well as the letters written to him by others. The earliest biography, <u>The Life of Saint Augustine</u>, was written not long after his death, by his friend Saint Possidius, the bishop of Calama. Possidius's text is generally held by historians to be quite credible.

Other biographies of Saint Augustine, both medieval and modern, tend to draw heavily from the works of Augustine and Possidius, although some draw also on legends. One such work with compilations about Augustine would be the 13th century <u>Lives of the Saints</u> by Jacobus de Voragine, archbishop of Genoa. Such works, while providing many interesting anecdotes, and reflections on the saint's character, are generally considered to be of lesser historical value.

A Young Augustine

Saint Augustine of Hippo was born in the year 354, in the city of Thagaste in the Numidia region of the Roman province called Africa. This city is today Souk Ahras, in Algeria.

Roman Africa at the time of Augustine's birth covered modern Tunisia and the Mediterranean coast of Libya and eastern Algeria. To the east it bordered the Roman province Cyrenaica, in western Egypt, and to the west it bordered on the Roman province Mauretania, which covered the Mediterranean coast of Morocco and much of Algeria.

Although with modern eyes it is easy to view Africa as a remote part of the Roman Empire, and to assume that it was a lesser province, the opposite is in fact true. In antiquity it was often more difficult to travel by land than by sea, so Roman Africa's position on the Mediterranean Sea put it right at the heart of the western Roman Empire. It was a flourishing and richly fertile province, often called "the granary of Rome" because without the grain imported from Africa the Italian cities would have succumbed to starvation.

Christianity was not quite yet the state religion of the Roman Empire at the time of Augustine's birth, but it certainly held a position of privilege. Long gone were the days of persecution for confessing a Christian faith. This, however, also meant that Christianity was divided, and persecution was being performed by Christians against Christians.

The Council of Nicaea was held in 325 to erase some of these divisions, proclaiming a unified Christian doctrine on the trinitarian nature of God, the nature of Jesus, and other things of great importance, such as the calculation of Easter. Unfortunately, such councils did little to unify the faith. Nor did it help that from 361, when Augustine was only seven years old, until 363, the pagan Emperor Julian set out to weaken the Church by granting unsupported divisions official approval. In Africa, this meant that the previously heretical Donatist faith, a very strict sect of Christians who revered martyrs, gained official status.

Thagaste, the city of Augustine's birth, lay sixty miles inland and was separated from the Mediterranean by the Medjera mountain range. Further south lay the mountains of Aures, which separate the Algerian plain from the Sahara desert. Even so, Thagaste had many of the elements of a busy harbor city. It lay on many inland roads used by merchants and travelers. Aside from Latin, Berber and Punic were languages that could be heard in the streets.

Augustine's father, Patricius, was a city official. He held the rank of *decurion*, a town councilor with tax collection duties. It was a position which Augustine, as the eldest son, was expected to inherit. In addition to his official government business, Patricius owned a vineyard, which was worked by several slaves. He was a pagan, and strongly opposed to having his children baptized. Augustine's mother, on the other hand, was called Monica. She is known to us now as Saint Monica. She was a Christian, and most likely of Berber heritage, and, like most Christians in Thagaste, she was a Donatist. After Augustine, she had two more children with Patricius: a son, Navigius, and a daughter, Perpetua.

Although there were many local languages in the Roman Empire, and Greek was both the prominent lingua franca and the language of the flourishing eastern empire, the language of Patricius and Monica's household was Latin. Patricius selected fluent Latin-speaking slaves and pedagogues for Augustine with his future, as an official of the western Roman Empire, in mind.

When Augustine was only eleven years old, he and his pedagogue, a type of slave who accompanies children in a parent's stead, were sent to live in the city of Madauros in order for Augustine to be close to a good school. It was a sophisticated intellectual and cultural center, where temples and churches of varying religions mingled. The pagan population of Madauros had recently increased in both size and vigor, thanks to Julian the Apostate, the pagan emperor who had died only two years before Augustine arrived.

The Blessed Augustine was not what one would call a good student. Free from parental oversight, he would often lie to his pedagogue and to his teachers about his whereabouts, and skip classes to attend the amphitheater. When he was forced to attend his classes, he was stubborn and often disinterested. Having been flogged many times for failing to learn Greek, the young Augustine simply decided that he would refuse to learn the language no matter how much he was beaten.

At other times, Augustine was deeply moved by his studies. In the time of Augustine's youth, all secular instruction, even when performed by Christians, used the Greek and Roman classics. These poems resonated with Augustine. "My ears were inflamed for pagan myths, and the more they were scratched the more they itched," he later wrote. He idolized Aeneas, the hero of Virgil's epic poem the *Aeneid*.

While in Madauros, Augustine made friends with several pagans. Among them was an older man by the name of Maximus, whom Augustine viewed as something of a mentor. Whether Augustine considered himself a pagan at this time in his life is difficult to say, but he did convince others, Maximus among them, that he was.

When Augustine turned sixteen he had finished his studies in Madauros and returned to his father's home in Thagaste. He was supposed to have started his rhetoric studies in Carthage that same year, but when the time came to pay for the tuition, Patricius could not produce the funds. Augustine took a gap year. A more studious person might have used his time to gain experiences through travel or work. Augustine, on the other hand, was not a studious person and sought experiences of another sort.

With his friends, Augustine roamed the streets of Thagaste after sunset, looking for just the right amount of trouble. "What was not allowed allured us," he wrote later of this year. After his conversion to Christianity, how he had stolen in those days simply for the sake of stealing came to haunt his conscience.

Sixteen was also the year when Augustine became sexually active. Horrified as she initially was, Saint Monica came to take quite a practical stance to her son's experimentation. Although she encouraged her son "with great anxiety" to stay chaste, she also made it clear to him that should he commit the sin of fornication, he must stay clear of married women. To Augustine, he later admitted, this was silly womanly advice, and at sixteen he would have been embarrassed to follow it.

We might have known nothing today of Augustine's youthful liaisons, if one of the women he bedded in that sixteenth year had not fallen pregnant. To spare her dignity, he simply called her *Una* when he wrote of her. The last thing that Augustine had wanted was to be tied down to a child. He was just getting started in life.

During his gap year he had caught the eye of Thagaste's most wealthy and influential man, Romanian. In addition to becoming Augustine's patron, Romanian took charge of his education and saw to it that Augustine would go to Carthage the following school year. In the meantime, Augustine spent a significant amount of his time on Romanian's estate. Some of that time was spent tutoring Romanian's two sons. In turn, and with the help of Romanian, the young rebellious Augustine, began to mature, but his maturity was short lived.

Augustine the Student, Augustine the Teacher

When Augustine left for rhetoric school in Carthage he took Una with him, and she lived there with him as his concubine. It was then, just before they left or soon after their arrival in Carthage, that Una gave birth to their son. His name was Adeodatus, meaning "Godsend."

Augustine was most unhappy about his newfound obligations and the commitment that he felt he had never signed up for. Amongst his classmates, he deeply admired the subversives. It was them that he chose to associate with, but not without a constant feeling of disconnect. He felt ashamed that he was unable to live up to their shamelessness, and to participate in their raids and pranks. When they spent their evenings roaming the city streets, Augustine was by necessity at home, studying through the night, to the frequent interruptions of his infant son.

During Augustine's first year at Carthage, his father died. Patricius reportedly converted to Christianity before dying, at the fervent request of his wife. Saint Monica stayed for some time in Thagaste, managing the estate. She must have visited Augustine and Una, and the baby Adeodatus, but although she was expected to move in with them she long put it off. The reason for this was that she did not approve of her son's sinful and heretical ways. In particular, they had many arguments on the topic of philosophy and Manichaeism.

When Augustine was nineteen, he came across, during his studies, a now lost dialogue of Cicero's called <u>Hortensius</u>. Having read it, he considered himself a convert of philosophy. The Christian scriptures of his mother seemed to him, when compared to philosophical treatises, unsophisticated, even crude.

As a result, Augustine was increasingly drawn to a group of people he had come to know over his first two years in Carthage: young, fun, Manichaean intellectuals. Augustine described their camaraderie with a heartfelt tenderness in his <u>Confessions</u>:

> Their other qualities more compelled my heart-conversation and laughter and mutual deferrings; shared readings of sweetly-phrased books, facetiousness alternating with things serious, heated arguing (as if with oneself), to spice our general agreement with dissent; teaching and being taught by turns; the

sadness at anyone's absence, and the joy of return. Reciprocated love for such semaphorings - a smile, a glance, a thousand winning acts - to fuse separate sparks into a single glow, no longer many souls but one.

Manichaeism, a gnostic religion revealed by its martyr-founder-prophet Mani, offered Augustine what he considered a rational cosmology, and detached enlightenment. Manichaeism preached a dualistic world inhabited by a Good God, whose God-particles inhabited all men, and an Evil God, constantly at battle with one another. Natural phenomena were the result of this divine battle. Even Creation itself was not a result of the actions of the Good God alone. The Earth and Mankind, they said, were both possessed by different ratios of Light and Dark. Manichaeism had room for Monica's Savior, whom Augustine had heard much of while attending the Donatist Church in Thagaste. Even the Trinity could be incorporated into Manichaeism, which preached a Trinity consisting of the Good God, the Light, who was Christ, and the Prophet Mani, the Messenger of the Light sent upon the World.

Further still, Manichaeism offered Augustine a chance to be the rebel he had always wanted, of which being an adolescent father and spouse had suddenly robbed him. Though not yet illegal, Manichaeism certainly had the flavor of the forbidden, as it was considered heretical by Christians, and greatly angered Monica. Even so, Saint Monica did eventually decide to look beyond her son's heretical views and moved in with him and Una.

Having finished his studies in Carthage, Augustine was called back to Thagaste by his patron Romanian to become a teacher. It is clear that by this time Romanian too had converted to Manichaeism, although not under the influence of Augustine. There were others, however, whose conversion to Manichaeism was strongly influenced by Augustine. He was a well-educated rhetorician who enjoyed debating, and gained quite a reputation as a proponent for intellectual Manichaeism.

After only two years of teaching in Thagaste, Augustine returned to Carthage to teach at his Alma Mater. It was in that time, during the year 380, when Augustine was 26 years old, that he published his first book. It was called <u>The Beautiful and the Appropriate</u>, but it is unfortunately lost to time.

While teaching in Carthage, Augustine also began to doubt the Manichaean faith he had often so eloquently defended to others. It seemed to Augustine that the cosmic myths proposed by Manichaeism failed to line up with the science and natural philosophy of the day.

What Augustine wanted was an intellectual teacher who could explain the discrepancies experienced by Augustine, and guide him back into faith. When Faustus, a renowned Manichaean speaker, came to Carthage Augustine sought him out. Although he was a charismatic leader, Faustus could not answer Augustine's most important questions in a satisfactory way.

He was not a well-read man like Augustine and was not familiar with the works that Augustine had been reading and teaching. Faustus was, however, open to learning and discussing, so the two men became good friends, although Augustine never did gain in Faustus the teacher he had hoped to find.

A Traveling Man

After only a few years in Carthage, Augustine decided to move on. He packed Monica, Una, and Adeodatus onto a boat and set sail for Rome, the city of his beloved masters, Virgil and Cicero.

When Augustine arrived in Rome, in 383, it was no longer the capital of the empire. The empire was divided in two parts, and the center of the western empire now lay in Milan. The golden age of Virgil that Augustine had hoped to find was long gone. Corrupt senators, who were as poor in scruples as they were rich in gold and land, ran the city. The city may have been pagan, but it lacked the heroic ethics of ancient pagan mythical poetry.

There was also much political instability in Italy when Augustine arrived. The same year, a popular general seized power from the western emperor, who had to flee to his eastern colleague for help to restore his power.

Although Augustine had been growing increasingly disillusioned with Manichaeism, he still used his Manichaean contacts to establish for himself a patron in Rome. Once there, however, he aligned himself with Quintus Aurelius Symmachus, a pagan senator of a fine old family who was famous for his oratory. Symmachus was also the prefect of the city, and part of an impressive circle of poets and other famous commentators Virgil. Augustine must have appreciated Symmachus's friends as much as he appreciated Symmachus himself.

The stay in Rome did not last long. Augustine was tired of teaching, worn thin by students frequently eluding payment, and unimpressed with Rome itself. Symmachus arranged for him a position at the court in Milan, as an official court orator. Augustine arrived at the imperial court in Milan in 384, when he was 30 years old.

In Milan, Augustine rose to a much higher social plateau. His household grew to include, aside from himself, Una, Saint Monica, and Adeodatus, his brother, two cousins, as well as several students, slaves, stenographers, and copyists.

Unlike Rome, Milan was a Christian city. At the time Augustine arrived it was split into two Christian fractions: Athanasians and Arians, who disagreed on the divinity of Jesus, and practical matters of ecclesiastical chastity and the dating of Easter. In Milan, these fractions were headed by the Catholic bishop Ambrose, now Saint Ambrose of Milan, and the Arian empress Justina respectively.

Whether Augustine felt any stronger affinity for any particular side is uncertain, but it is clear that he did not particularly seek out Ambrose, and his conversion is unlikely to have been influenced by the same. Saint Ambrose was not opposed to using miracles as a means of gaining popular support, and Augustine in those early years was deeply skeptical towards miracles, as they were used frequently in his mother's Donatist faith.

Although they were both present at the court, Augustine only called on Saint Ambrose twice: once as a courtesy call when he arrived at court, and then once again to ask him about fasting in Milan, on Saint Monica's behalf. For Augustine's part, he probably had as much trouble relating to the bishop as the bishop had to him. Augustine tells us that Saint Ambrose suggested to him a reading from Isaiah, completely oblivious to the fact that the unbaptized Augustine would have had no familiarity with the symbolic reading of Scripture. In his literal reading of the Bible, the younger Augustine could not understand Isaiah at all.

With his new well-paid position at court, and being now a grown man, Augustine was quickly becoming a very eligible bachelor. Saint Monica, who was still managing her husband's estate, arranged for Augustine to be engaged to a Christian heiress of not yet marriageable age. The fact that she was not yet marriageable indicates to us that she must have been less than twelve years old, to Augustine's thirty.

The fact that Monica did not arrange for Augustine to marry Una may indicate that there was a difference in class between them, which would have made it impossible for the two to legally marry. Perhaps Una was not the right kind of Christian. It is also possible that Una had grown weary of her relationship with Augustine. He was a heretic, for one thing, but they also clearly wanted different things out of the relationship. Augustine has indicated in his own writings that he used contraceptive strategies against Una's wishes. Maybe Una relented for the sake of her son, Adeodatus. If she could not marry Augustine, he could still adopt Adeodatus with his wife, and thus legitimize the child's birth.

Even so, they had been together for fourteen years and it was not an easy separation to bear. Augustine wrote about the pain he experienced when Una left. "Since she was an obstacle to my marriage, the woman I lived with for so long was torn out of my side," he wrote. "My heart, to which she had been grafted, was lacerated, wounded, shedding blood." The heartache, it seems, was not enough for him to stay celibate until he married his young fiancée. Augustine promptly took a new concubine.

The Conversion

In Milan, Augustine met Saint Simplician, a mentor of Saint Ambrose who had been elected his teacher of doctrine. The two men struck up a friendship and Saint Simplician frequently received Augustine for long discussions. He introduced Augustine to a budding Neo-Platonist Christian community in Milan, which of course spoke to Augustine's philosophical leanings.

Simplician also had the sensitivity to understand what Augustine needed, and when he needed it. He provided him with stories of conversion, flavored to Augustine's sensibilities, and recommended scripture readings that Augustine could relate to. While Ambrose had suggested a symbolic reading, Simplician guided Augustine towards the writings of Paul, whose clear and direct message he could better grasp.

Simplician's conversion stories inspired Augustine in much the same way that Latin poetry once had. He saw himself as the heroes of these stories and wanted to go through what they had gone through. At the same time, he felt a weakness of will. As much as he desired to be like one of these men, he could not find the power to break away from the contrary life he was leading, with his wealth, and his mistress.

His own contradictory nature was an escalating crisis for Augustine. It all happened to come tumbling down around him one day in 386 as he was walking in a garden, with his friend Alypius. What he experienced was akin to a panic attack. He could control his physical body – pull his hair, hug his knees – but he could not control his will, and free himself from slavery to his habits.

He saw then, with his mind's eye, self-control embodied in female form. She reached out to him, to embrace him, and in her arms were multitudes of good examples. Lady Self-Control said to him:

> Canst not thou what these youths, what these maidens can? Or can they either in themselves, and not rather in the Lord their God? The Lord their God gave me unto them. Why standest thou in thyself, and so standest not? Cast thyself upon Him, fear not, He will not withdraw Himself that thou shouldest fall; cast thyself fearlessly upon Him, He will receive, and will heal thee.

Next, Augustine saw himself walking into the desert, where he sat beneath a fig tree. In both that place and in the garden, where Alypius sat by him, he wept and he spoke of his heart's repentance. That is when he heard the chanting voice of a child. He assumed that it came from a nearby house, but it surprised him. It seemed to chant "Take up and read," but Augustine's experience told him that no child would be happy to chant such a thing.

He took it to be a command from God and arose immediately to retrieve a Latin translation of the Gospels, which he brought back to the place where Alypius was still sitting. He opened the book and read that section on which his eyes first fell. It was Romans 13: "not in orgies and drunkenness, not in promiscuity and licentiousness, not in rivalry and jealousy. But put on the Lord Jesus Christ, and make no provision for the desires of the flesh."

There he stopped, for as Augustine himself put it: "instantly at the end of this sentence, by a light as it were of serenity infused into my heart, all the darkness of doubt vanished away."

Augustine decided that he would not simply be a Christian, he was going to be a Christian ascetic. This in itself is not greatly surprising. Asceticism was a popular philosophical ideal in late antiquity. It was upheld both by pagans and by Manichaeans, but it was a state maintained only by the most serious of practitioners.

As a Manichaean, Augustine had been content with being a layperson with wealth and ties to the secular world. As a Christian, Augustine wanted more. He would leave his prominent position at the court, and give up his fiancée, but first he would be baptized, along with his friend Alypius and his son Adeodatus, during Holy Week of 387.

While waiting to be initiated into the Christian mysteries, Augustine wrote four dialogues. These early dialogues were of course Christian in nature, but contained no commentary on the scriptures. That may have been because Augustine was not yet initiated into the mysteries. Writing about them would have been, simply put, presumptuous.

Augustine's first introduction to the symbolic reading of the scriptures came through Saint Ambrose's instructions to candidates for baptism.

In his instructions, Ambrose traced the spiritual bath of baptism back to Noah's flood, to the passage of the Red Sea, to Jesus healing a blind man in the pool of Siloam, to the waters that Moses sweetened, and to the water that floated the ax of Elijah.

On the more practical side of things, candidates were expected to spend all of Lent unbathed and wearing penitential hair suits. They were assigned a special place in the church, and had to memorize the Apostle's Creed and Lord's Prayer.

On Thursday of Holy Week they were finally allowed to bathe, and were submitted to a physical examination. On Easter Eve they prayed through the night, renounced Satan at dawn, turned to the sun, and were conducted to the octagonal pool for baptism.

After his baptism at the Church of Saint John the Baptist in Milan, Augustine returned to Rome where he no doubt settled into the city's Christian community. At Rome he wrote two more dialogues, as well as a treatise on Catholic and Manichaean moral systems. But his heart was always in Africa, and it was there he wished to go. In 388 he set sail for the second, and final, time in his life. Before their travels took them to their homeland, however, Saint Monica, passed away.

Preaching in Africa

When he arrived in Thagaste, Augustine resettled on his father's property and accepted, for a while, the duties of a decurion, the job and station he inherited from his father. Una had probably been living in Thagaste for several years at this point, and it is likely that Adeodatus was in contact with her, but Augustine never wrote of her again. Their son was at this time sixteen, and featured in his father's newly penned dialogue The Teacher. Tragically, Adeodatus died suddenly of unknown causes the same year.

Where he had once debated in favor of Manichaeism, Augustine was now debating for Christianity. His rising reputation as a rhetorician and orator meant that he now had to be careful in his travels – not because someone might accost him, but because someone may shanghai him into becoming a priest or a bishop. At the time, churches in the western Roman Empire had a tendency of pronouncing any visiting scholar their new priest or bishop, with or without their consent. Saint Ambrose had been appointed bishop in much the same way without even being baptized.

But Augustine did not want to stay in Thagaste, so he set his sight on Hippo Regius. That city already had bishop, and by ecclesiastical law the bishop was the only one allowed to preach there. There was therefore no conceivable way for Augustine to be forced off the ascetic path that he had chosen for himself. There was also a community of monks in Hippo, whom Augustine wanted to join.

The bishop of Hippo was a man called Valerius. According to Augustine's biographer, Possidius, he was "a Greek by birth and less versed in the Latin language and literature." This was most unfortunate for Augustine, for Valerius was a man quite aware of his failings. He decided that he would like Augustine, a man of rhetoric and Latin, to take on the preaching at Hippo.

This went against all of Augustine's wishes for a peaceful ascetic life. He resisted the request, argued that it was against the law and that he needed to study rather than to teach, but Valerius was more than willing to work around such problems. He offered Augustine plenty of time to study, absolved him of the interdiction on preaching, and promised a garden next to the church to create a monastic community in lieu of that he would be leaving. Augustine simply could not say no.

Thus he became the presbyter of Hippo Regius.

The monastic community that Augustine created was meant to imitate the manner and rule of the holy apostles. Its principal rule was that no man should have possessions of his own, but rather all things should be communal and distributed to each according to his need.

Augustine preached to the Catholics of Hippo between 391 and 396. He was an engaging speaker and his lively sermons, full of wit, pun, and wordplay, were very popular. They did, however, draw some criticism from those who felt that Augustine was pandering to the uncivilized mob, rather than raising them up.

In the year 393, Valerius had Augustine address the African bishops during the pan-African council. It was most likely there that Augustine first met the primate of Carthage, Bishop Aurelius. He was a reformer with grand plans, and he quite enjoyed Augustine's address of faith and creed. The two of them struck up a partnership with the intent of remaking African Christianity over the course of several decades. Augustine would train, in his monastery, the bishops that Aurelius would then strategically place into parishes.

As Augustine's influence in Hippo grew, so did his confidence and his desire to unite all Christians under the banner of Catholicism. He wanted to meet the Donatists head on and win the people over with public debates. His rhetoric was well known and he was set to win. Unfortunately, the Donatists were not interested in public debates. They were not interested in sharing any sort of space with Catholics at all, who they considered to be sinners. The animosity was such that Donatists refused to greet Catholics in public and would not do business with them.

For all of the distaste that Augustine had felt for the Donatists over the years, he also admired them. They were extremely strict and very harsh towards any sinfulness. Augustine, with his long held ascetic ideals, approved of this and he hoped to fashion Catholicism a bit closer to Donatism.

One such push to bring Catholicism closer to Donatism occurred in 395, around the feast day of Hippo's first martyr-saint. Bishop Valerius had already ordered the Catholic community not to engage in their usual drunken festivity, which had made him incredibly unpopular. Augustine followed the bishop's speech with three days of hellfire-and-doom addresses, right before the saint's feast day. The first of the speeches was very poorly received, the second was not much better, but by the end of the third day the celebrations were canceled. The Catholics would hold a sombre, and sober, celebration.

Although the Donatists would not debate with him, Augustine did have the chance to meet his former Manichaean brothers in verbal battle. Possidius tells us of one such event.

In Hippo, many men had been swayed over to Manichaeism by the preaching of a Manichaean presbyter by the name of Fortunatus. Catholics and Donatists alike urged Augustine to debate with this man, but Fortunatus was familiar with Augustine from the days when they were both Manichaeans and did not particularly wish butt heads.

Eventually, however, Fortunatus was shamed by his fellow Manichaeans into meeting Augustine in the debate. He left the debate even more shamed, having been unable to challenge Augustine at all, and never returned to Hippo.

Bishop of Hippo

Augustine's sermons, in particular those held on sobriety in conjunction with the saint's day in 395, had soon secured Augustine a place as one of the most influential men in Hippo. Afraid that his reformer preacher would be snatched up by another diocese with an opening, Valerius did something unprecedented: he wrote to the primate of Carthage and requested that Hippo be granted not one, but two bishops. himself and Augustine together. Augustine was first made coadjutor bishop, and then fully consecrated in 395, forty-one years old, only four years after becoming a priest, and only eight years after his baptism.

In 397, when Augustine had been a bishop for only two years, he started writing his <u>Confessions,</u> in which he explored his own inner mind. To Augustine, this was one way in which he could come to better understand God. Humans, the Bible states, were made in the image of God, and so, Augustine thought, the human mind must also reflect God's mind. Aside from his confessions, Augustine also threw himself into writing <u>On Christian Doctrine</u>, which would take years to complete.

These were busy years for Augustine. He was also preaching and holding councils on reformation of African Christianity, in addition to being burdened with a high number of secular duties that were increasingly being foisted onto clergy. As part of these duties he was acting as a secular judge. He was also still the leader of his monastic community.

Despite of his high standing, Augustine remained true to his ideals. His clothing and footwear were always modest, neither too fine nor too coarse. The bedclothes of his community were equally modest, sufficient but no more. The food served was frugal, but guests and brothers suffering from illness or fatigue could expect to be served meat from time to time.

Augustine avoided spending time alone with women as well as having women under his roof. It was not simply because of his own prior inability to control his lusts, but also because he was in the public eye and did not want to invite any rumors. Even his sister, a widow who had devoted herself to God, was not allowed to live with him. Rather, handmaidens cared her for in her own house. His nieces who likewise had made vows to God were often kept at a necessary arm's length.

In 410, the Visigoth leader Alaric captured the city of Rome. The shock waves of this event were felt throughout the entire empire. The Roman Empire, with the city itself at the center, was generally felt to be permanent and unconquerable. But the effects felt in Africa were not merely emotional. Although Alaric was a Christian, he was of the Arian persuasion, so Catholics from all over the western Roman Empire poured into Africa, fearing what may happen to them under the Arians.

The times were most definitely uncertain. In Africa, it was also a time of heightened violence and clashes between Donatists and Catholics. Emperor Honarius therefore sent a tribune to Africa to settle the question once and for all. Donatism and Catholicism would meet in officially sanctioned debates, and whichever side was proclaimed the victor would have the legal faith.

Augustine was strongly in favor of this imperial involvement. He had, after all, been trying to get the Donatists to debate him for some time. In order to show them good will, he turned to the Catholic bishops in order to issue a joint agreement. It stated that the Catholics would approve of any ruling the Emperor's tribune made, even surrendering their churches if they were found to have the unlawful faith. In case they were proclaimed the winners, however, they would still allow Donatists to keep their offices, letting Donatist bishops be Catholic bishops. The Donatists for their part made no such gesture.

At the initial meeting, the Donatists made a great show of numbers, calling upon as many of their Bishops to attend as possible, and trying to keep down the number of Catholics in attendance by publicly questioning the way they had been consecrated. Among those rejected were, of course, Augustine, having been appointed to a city where there already was a Bishop. The final count showed 284 Donatist bishops to 286 Catholics.

Each side was told to choose seven speakers, seven advisers or researchers to back them up, and four men to keep records. Even so, the Donatists all showed up *en masse* on the opening day of discussions, and demanded to all be received. They then refused to sit down with sinners. Marcellinus, the tribune, was a layman and could not sit down while Bishops were standing, so he had to conduct the entire hearing on his feet.

The Donatists had further demands. They required all bishops to show credentials, so that everyone could tell that they were truly allowed to represent their local church. They also demanded that reports be taken in long-hand, so that they could easily see if reporting was done accurately. Many of the Catholic bishops, it turned out during these proceedings, were illiterate.

Augustine, Aurelius, and Alypius were all among those chosen to speak for the Catholics, and it was hard for the Donatists to try to match these men's rhetorical, legal, and organizational wisdom. Commentators have argued that there was little evidence of organization at all in the Donatist defense. They focused rather on delaying, obstructing, and questioning their opponents' legitimacy, than on arguing for their cause. As Augustine spoke, they heckled him, shouted, and tried to make sure that he was not heard. Alypius, a true lawyer, the record shows, proclaimed, "Let the record show that they are interrupting him."

On June 26, 411, Marcellinus made his decision. Donatists were officially heretics, and not allowed to own churches, hold offices or have meetings. They were also to be fined for not attending Catholic Church. Enforcement, however, was patchy at best. Fines were hard to collect, and some leading Donatists managed to hold onto their churches for a whole decade after the edict. Violent resistance occurred and a number of Catholic priests were mutilated or murdered.

In all of this, Augustine was still a proponent of peace. He did not want the Donatists harmed, and again he promised their bishops that they would retain their offices if they came into the Catholic Church. He would himself preach in his Basilica on alternating weeks, sharing the duty with the Donatist bishop in Hippo. Many contemporaries found Augustine far too lenient in this matter.

It was during this time that Augustine was working on The City of God, one of his most important works. At the same time, he was putting the finishing touches on another of his greatest works, On the Trinity, which he had begun a full decade earlier.

Much of Augustine's time must have been taken up by the writing and dictation of letters. When he could not attend public debates in person, he took them up in letter. Throughout 412 he wrote intensively on the subject of the heresies of Pelagius, which were gaining popularity in Africa. He exchanged several letters with Saint Jerome, and for years he maintained a lengthy argument with Bishop Julian of Eclanum entirely by letter. More than 250 of Saint Augustine's letters remain today.

By 418, Augustine had clearly become an international celebrity. He was asked by Pope Zosimus to lead a panel of African bishops in settling an ecclesiastical conflict in the neighboring province, Mauretani.

The Final Years

In the 420s, a new wave of relics came from the Holy Land, along with miracles. The world was changing. Augustine was slowing down. He turned over many of his duties, and set about revising his books. It was not simply a matter of changing opinions, but growing understanding as well. There were works that he had composed while a layman, or early in his ecclesiastical career, and less educated in scripture or the nature of God.

Those works he took it upon himself to either censor or update. This was something that he could do with relative effectiveness, because Augustine closely guarded the copying of his books. In antiquity, books had to be copied by hand and was usually done so far out of the reach of the author. Often, only select bits were copied. But, for most part, Augustine preferred to have people write to him for copies of his books so that he could control the contents.

Like the Visigoths had descended upon Italy, twenty years earlier, the Vandals descended upon Africa. One by one the cities fell to the Arian Vandals. People flocked to Hippo Regius, as it was a fortified city. Unfortunately, this was not enough to keep them safe. The Vandals besieged the city for over a year.

Augustine was by this time already very ill, but the nature of his illness or at what time it first showed itself is not known. He saw his own sickness and how it would take him, and preferred that it did so sooner rather than later. In response to the Vandal siege, he prayed with his brothers:

> I would have you know that in this time of our misfortune I ask this of God: either that He may be pleased to free this city which is surrounded by the foe, or if something else seems good in His sight, that He make His servants brave for enduring His will, or at least that He may take me from this world unto Himself.

Augustine's health declined rapidly during the siege, and he found himself confined to his bed. This must have been terribly frustrating for a man who had always been incredibly busy, in both mind and body. When a stranger came to his bedside to be healed, he told him that if he had any power to heal anyone, surely, the stranger must understand, that he would have already healed himself. But the stranger told him that God had spoken to him in a dream, and told him to come to Augustine. And so, as by a miracle, Augustine lay his hands on the sickly man and healed him.

Alas, Augustine could not heal himself. His prayer was answered on August 28, 430. He was taken from this life, and from the besieged city of Hippo, at age 76.

In his last days, Augustine was confined to bed. He had asked his monks to copy for him the penitential psalms of David. They hung from the wall next to his bed, so that he may read them and repent. To do this, he asked that no one came to him except when the physician would come to check on him or a brother came to feed him. He wept openly and constantly.

Augustine was buried in Hippo. According to the True Martyrology, by the Venerable Bede, the body of the saint was later moved to Sardinia by Catholic bishops fleeing Africa after the invasion of the Vandals.

The body was moved once more in the 8th century, to Pavia in northern Italy, where it was thought the relics of the saint would be safe from Muslim raiders. There the body of Augustine remained until the early 18th century, when it was moved to Milan. The remains of Augustine have since been reinstated in Pavia.

The miracles of Saint Augustine after his death were not reported by Saint Possidius. They remain rather in the compilations of saint legends. One such miracle relates to the relics of Saint Augustine.

A man with particularly great devotion to Saint Augustine, it is said in Lives of the Saints, paid a monk a great sum for the finger of the saint. Fingers were a popular relic at the time, so this in itself was not terribly uncommon.

The monk, however, took the man's money and gave him, instead of the finger of the saint, the finger of an unknown dead man, wrapped in silk. The buyer received it with great reverence and honored the relic daily. Because he was a good and faithful man, God decided to set right this malicious deed and replaced the finger with Augustine's, after which several miracles were worked.

When word came to the abbey that this good man had the finger of Augustine, the monk swore to the abbot that he had sold him another man's finger. Yet, when they opened the tomb of Saint Augustine the finger was missing.

Seeker, Speaker, Saint

Although he taught on the nature of God, and although he led many into his open arms, Saint Augustine was forever a spiritual seeker. His desire to understand the world around him, his desire for virtue, and his desire for logic, urged him on a winding path.

It caused him to rejoice in the pagan classics, whose leading men battled with nature and showed great heroic virtue. It caused him to see the beauty in reasoning and asking difficult questions, as philosophy did, and it let him take on the world view of the Manichaeans. It likewise caused him to keep asking questions, to look at science, to shun and to fall away from that same faith. Having finally found a home in the Catholic Church, his desires kept urging him into deeper contemplation, and further seeking into the nature of the Divine.

Like so many with a seeking and questioning nature, Augustine had trouble accepting the faith of his childhood, which he had so strongly rejected in his formative years. Yet, when the need was strong, it was right there waiting for him. In the meantime, however, Augustine's rejection of Christianity colored his relationship with his Christian parent. Her influence on him and his faith was sadly something that Augustine never truly understood or appreciated until she had already passed away. His mother's profound influence on him was something he came to treasure in later years.

If Augustine was a seeker foremost, then he was a speaker second. Having received an education in rhetoric certainly helped, but Augustine's reputation implies also a strong natural inclination. He was a successful teacher, and even as a Manichaean he was a strong debater and is known to have created converts for that religion with his speeches. As a Christian, his ability to speak propelled him into the public eye. Had he not been an excellent orator, it is doubtful that we would have known anything about Saint Augustine at all.

But, it was not his high brow orations that made Augustine an excellent speaker. It was his ability to relate to the listener. Certainly, he was known for his verbal fireworks, the little extras that amaze the crowd, but it was his use of popular language, slang, witticisms, and puns that drew the people to him. Augustine could read the crowd and speak to them in a way that appealed to them.

Augustine the saint was a humble man who did not proclaim to work miracles. When a man came to him with a sickly relative, asking to be healed, Augustine himself said that he was not a healer. It was only when the man told him that he had heard God's voice telling him that Augustine could heal his relative that Augustine did God's will and healed the sick man. Although, by the time of this event, Augustine changed his opinion on the prevalence of miracles, his early position on miracles was one of skepticism.

Because Augustine lived in the 4th and 5th century, a time when saints were proclaimed by the Catholic people rather than by the Pope, Saint Augustine has never been officially canonized. He was however recognized as a Doctor of the Church in 1298, by Pope Boniface VIII. He is the patron saint of theologians, printers, and brewers. His feast day is on August 28 in the Catholic Church, on June 15 in the Eastern Orthodox Church, and on November 4 in the Assyrian Church of the East.

Prayers by Saint Augustine

Faith is to believe what you do not see; the reward of this faith is to see what you believe.

Act of Hope

For your mercies' sake, O Lord my God, tell me what you are to me.

Say to my soul: "I am your salvation."

So speak that I may hear, O Lord; my heart is listening; open it that it may hear you, and say to my soul: "I am your salvation."

After hearing this word, may I come in haste to take hold of you.

Hide not your face from me.

Let me see your face even if I die, lest I die with longing to see it.

The house of my soul is too small to receive you; let it be enlarged by you.

It is all in ruins; do you repair it.

There are thing in it - I confess and I know - that must offend your sight.

But who shall cleanse it? Or to what others besides you shall I cry out?

From my secret sins cleanse me, O Lord, and from those of others spare your servant.

Amen.

Act of Petition

Give me yourself, O my God, give yourself to me.

Behold I love you, and if my love is too weak a thing,
grant me to love you more strongly.
I cannot measure my love to know how much it falls short of being
sufficient, but let my soul hasten to your embrace and never be turned
away until it is hidden in the secret shelter of your presence.
This only do I know, that it is not good for me when you are not with
me, when you are only outside me. I want you in my very self.
All the plenty in the world which is not my God is utter want.
Amen.

Breathe in Me, Holy Spirit

Breathe in me O Holy Spirit, that my thoughts may all be holy;

Act in me O Holy Spirit, that my work, too, may be holy;
Draw my heart O Holy Spirit, that I love but what is holy;
Strengthen me O Holy Spirit, to defend all that is holy;
Guard me, then, O Holy Spirit, that I always may be holy.
Amen.

Lord Jesus, Let Me Know Myself

Lord Jesus, let me know myself and know You,

And desire nothing save only You.
Let me hate myself and love You.
Let me do everything for the sake of You.
Let me humble myself and exalt You.
Let me think of nothing except You.
Let me die to myself and live in You.
Let me accept whatever happens as from You.
Let me banish self and follow You,
And ever desire to follow You.
Let me fly from myself and take refuge in You,
That I may deserve to be defended by You.
Let me fear for myself, let me fear You,
And let me be among those who are chosen by You.
Let me distrust myself and put my trust in You.
Let me be willing to obey for the sake of You.
Let me cling to nothing save only to You,
And let me be poor because of You.
Look upon me, that I may love You.
Call me that I may see You,
And for ever enjoy You.
Amen.

Prayer for the Indwelling of the Spirit

Holy Spirit, powerful Consoler, sacred Bond of the Father and the Son, Hope of the afflicted, descend into my heart and establish in it your loving dominion. Enkindle in my tepid soul the fire of your Love so that I may be wholly subject to you. We believe that when you dwell in us, yolu also prepare a dwelling for the Father and the Son. Deign, therefore, to come to me, Consoler of abandoned souls, and Protector of the needy. Help the afflicted, strengthen the weak, and support the wavering. Come and purify me.

Let no evil desire take possession of me. You love the humble and resist the proud. Come to me, glory of the living, and hope of the dying. Lead me by your grace that I may always be pleasing to you. Amen.

Prayer for the Sick

Watch, O Lord, with those who wake, or watch, or weep tonight,
and give your angels charge over those who sleep.
Tend your sick ones, O Lord Christ.
Rest your weary ones.
Bless your dying ones.
Soothe your suffering ones.
Pity your afflicted ones.
Shield your joyous ones.
And for all your love's sake.
Amen.

Prayer of Joy at the Birth of Jesus

Let the just rejoice, for their Justifict is born.

Let the sick and infirm rejoice, for their Savior is born.
Let the captives rejoice, for their Redeemer is born.
Let slaves rejoice, for their Master is born.
Let free people rejoice, for their Liberator is born.
Let all Christians rejoice, for Jesus Christ is born.

Amen.

Prayer of Trust in God's Heavenly Promise

My God, let me know and love you, so that I may find my happiness in you. Since I cannot fully achieve this on earth, help me to improve daily until I may do so to the full Enable me to know you ever more on earth, so that I may know you perfectly in heaven. Enable me to love you ever more on earth, so that I may love you perfectly in heave. In that way my joy may be great on earth, and perfect with you in heaven.

O God of truth, grant me the happiness of heaven so that my joy may be full in accord with your promise. In the meantime let my mind dwell on that happiness, my tongue speak of it, my heart pine for it, my mouth pronounce it, my soul hunger for it, my flesh thirst for it, and my entire being desire it until I enter through death in the joy of my Lord forever.
Amen.

Prayer on Finding God after a Long Search

Too late have I loved you, O Beauty so ancient, O Beauty so new.

Too late have I loved you!
You were within me but I was outside myself, and there I sought you!
In my weakness I ran after the beauty of the things you have made.
You were with me, and I was not with you.
The things you have made kept me from you - the things which would
have no being unless they existed in you!
You have called, you have cried, and you have pierced my deafness.
You have radiated forth, you have shined out brightly,
and you have dispelled my blindness.
You have sent forth your fragrance, and I have breathed it in, and I
long for you.
I have tasted you, and I hunger and thirst for you.
You have touched me, and I ardently desire your peace.
Amen.

Prayer to Our Lady, Mother of Mercy

Blessed Virgin Mary, who can worthily repay you with praise and thanks for having rescued a fallen world by your generous consent! Receive our gratitude, and by your prayers obtain the pardon of our sins. Take our prayers into the sanctuary of heaven and enable them to make our peace with God.

Holy Mary, help the miserable, strengthen the discouraged, comfort the sorrowful, pray for your people, plead for the clergy, intercede for all women consecrated to God. May all who venerate you feel now your help and protection. Be ready to help us when we pray, and bring back to us the answers to our prayers. Make it your continual concern to pray for the people of God, foryou were blessed by God and were made worthy to bear the Redeemer of the world, who lives and reigns forever. Amen.

Prayer to Seek God Continually

O Lord my God, I believe in you, Father, Son and Holy Spirit.

Insofar as I can, insofar as you have given me the power, I have sought you. I became weary and I labored.

O Lord my God, my sole hope, help me to believe and never to cease seeking you. Grant that I may always and ardently seek out your countenance. Give me the strength to seek you, for you help me to find you and you have more and more given me the hope of finding you.

Here I am before you with my firmness and my infirmity. Preserve the first and heal the second.

Here I am before you with my strength and my ignorance. Where you have opened the door to me, welcome me at the entrance; where you have closed the door to me, open to my cry; enable me to remember you, to understand you, and to love you. Amen.

Watch, O Lord

Watch, O Lord, with those who wake, or watch, or weep tonight,
and give Your angels and saints charge over those who sleep.
Tend Your sick ones, O Lord Christ. Rest Your weary ones.
Bless Your dying ones.
Soothe Your suffering ones.
Pity Your afflicted ones.
Shield Your joyous ones, and all for Your love's sake.
Amen.

You are Christ

You are Christ,

my Holy Father,
my Tender God,
my Great King,
my Good Shepherd,
my Only Master,
my Best Helper,
my Most Beautiful and my Beloved,
my Living Bread,
my Priest Forever,
my Leader to my Country,
my True Light,
my Holy Sweetness,
my Straight Way,
my Excellent Wisdom,
my Pure Simplicity,
my Peaceful Harmony,
my Entire Protection,
my Good Portion,
my Everlasting Salvation.

Christ Jesus, Sweet Lord,
why have I ever loved,
why in my whole life
have I ever desired anything except You,
Jesus my God?
Where was I when I was not in spirit with You?
Now, from this time forth,
do you, all my desires, grow hot,
and flow out upon the Lord Jesus:
run... you have been tardy until now;
hasten where you are going;
seek Whom you are seeking.
O, Jesus may he who loves You
not be an anathema;

may he who loves You
not be filled with bitterness.

O, Sweet Jesus,
may every good feeling that is fitted for Your praise,
love You, delight in You, adore You!
God of my heart,
and my Portion, Christ Jesus,
may my heart faint away in spirit,
and may You be my Life within me!
May the live coal of Your Love
grow hot within my spirit
and break forth into a perfect fire;
may it burn incessantly on the altar of my heart;
may it glow in my innermost being;
may it blaze in hidden recesses of my soul;
and in the days of my consummation
may I be found consummated with You!

Amen.

Prayers to Saint Augustine

Prayer I

Beloved Saint of our age, Saint Augustine, you were at first wholly human-centered and attached to false teachings.

Finally converted through God's grace, you became a praying theologian -- God-centered, God-loving, and God-preaching.

Help theologians in their study of revealed truth.

Let them always follow the Church Magisterium as they strive to communicate traditional teachings in a new form that will appeal to our contemporaries.

Amen.

Litany to Saint Augustine

Lord, have mercy on us.

Christ, have mercy on us.

Lord, have mercy on us. Christ, hear us.
Christ, graciously hear us.

God the Father of Heaven,
Have mercy on us.

God the Son, Redeemer of the world,
Have mercy on us.

God the Holy Ghost,
Have mercy on us.

Holy Trinity, One God,
Have mercy on us.

Holy Mary,
pray for us.

Holy Mother of God,
pray for us.

Holy Virgin of virgins,
pray for us.

Holy Father Augustine,
pray for us.

Saint Augustine, example of contrite souls,
pray for us.

St. Augustine, son of the tears of thy mother Monica,
pray for us.

St. Augustine, light of teachers,
pray for us.

St. Augustine, exterminator of heresies,
pray for us.

St. Augustine, illustrious warrior against the foes of the Church,
pray for us.

St. Augustine, pillar of the True Faith,
pray for us.

St. Augustine, vessel of Divine Wisdom,
pray for us.

St. Augustine, rule of conduct for apostolic life,
pray for us.

St. Augustine, whose heart was inflamed with the fire of Divine Love,
pray for us.

St. Augustine, humble and merciful father,
pray for us.

St. Augustine, zealous preacher of the Word of God,
pray for us.

St. Augustine, illumined expounder of Sacred Scripture,
pray for us.

St. Augustine, ornament of bishops,
pray for us.

St. Augustine, light of the True Faith,
pray for us.

St. Augustine, noble defender of Holy Church,
pray for us.

St. Augustine, refulgence of the glory of God,
pray for us.

St. Augustine, blossoming olive tree of the House of God,
pray for us.

St. Augustine, indefatigable adorer of the Most Holy Trinity,
pray for us.

St. Augustine, inexhaustible fountain of Christian eloquence,
pray for us.

St. Augustine, shining mirror of holiness,
pray for us.

St. Augustine, model of all virtues,
pray for us.

St. Augustine, consoler of the distressed,
pray for us.

St. Augustine, comforter of the forsaken,
pray for us.

St. Augustine, friend and helper of the poor,
pray for us.

St. Augustine, our father,
pray for us.

Lamb of God, Who takest away the sins of the world,
Spare us, O Lord.

Lamb of God, Who takest away the sins of the world,
Graciously hear us, O Lord.

Lamb of God, Who takest away the sins of the world,
Have mercy on us, O Lord.

Christ, hear us.

Christ, graciously hear us.

Let Us Pray

O God, Who didst disclose to Saint Augustine
the hidden mysteries of Thy wisdom
and didst enkindle in his heart
the flame of Divine Love,
thus renewing in Thy Church
the pillar of cloud and fire,
graciously grant that we may pass safely
through the storms of this world
and reach the eternal fatherland
which Thou didst promise us,
through Christ Our Lord.

Amen

49177043R00046

Made in the USA
Middletown, DE
18 June 2019